PLACES APART

# LOUGH DERG

Eileen Good

Photography by Anne Cassidy

VERITAS

First published 2003 by
Veritas Publications
7/8 Lower Abbey Street
Dublin 1
Ireland
Email publications@veritas.ie
Website www.veritas.ie

ISBN 1 85390 6883

10 9 8 7 6 5 4 3 2 1

Copyright © Veritas Publications

**Acknowledgements**

'Bless to Us, O God' from *The Iona Community Worship Book,* 1996 The Iona Community, published by Wild Goose Publications, Glasgow G2 3DH, Scotland; used with permission. 'In the Depths of Silence' by Indonesian author reproduced by kind permission of SPCK. Extracts from *Patrick The Pilgrim Apostle of Ireland* by Maire B. de Paor (Veritas Publications). 'Soul of Ireland' by Tom Renaud from *Forefront,* Summer 1999, (Spiritual Life Institute, Holy Hill Hermitage, Skreen, Co. Sligo); used with permission. Prayer from *A Lenten Journey* by Donal Neary, S.J., 'Station Island, Lough Derg' by Simon Kennedy from *Pilgrims' Tales ... And More,* eds. Mary McDaid and Pat McHugh and extract from *No Earthly Estate. God and Patrick Kavanagh: An anthology,* ed.Tom Stack. All published by Columba Press. Used with permission. Extracts from *Lough Derg* by Patrick Kavanagh are reprinted with the permission of the Trustees of the Estate of the late Katherine B. Kavanagh, through the Jonathan Williams Literary Agency. 'The Pilgrim' by Brendan Kennelly from *The Boats are Home* (Bloodaxe). 'The Pilgrim Prayer' © Ballintubber Abbey Trust, 1999. Extracts from *The New Dictionary of Theology* by Joseph A. Komonchat, Mary Collins and Dermot A. Lane (The Liturgical Press, Minnesota, USA). Extract from *Patrick in his own words* by Bishop Joseph Duffy, extract from *The Experience of God: An Invitation to Do Theology* by Dermot A. Lane, and 'I Light A Candle' by Ruth Patterson from *A Farther Shore* and 'Lord, thank you that you are a pilgrim God' – by Ruth Patterson from *Journeys Towards Reconciliation: A Song for Ireland* all published by Veritas Publications. 'Stay with me' and 'In our darkness' songs from Taizé © Ateliers et Presses de Taizé, Taizé-Community, France; used with permission. 'The Night' and 'The Rosary' by John O'Donohue from *Conamara Blues* published by Bantam. Used by permission of Transworld Publishers, a division of The Random House Group Ltd. Psalm 31, translation copyright © 1963, 1986, 1993 The Grail (England). 'Resurrection' by Vladimir Holan (1905-1980), translated by George Theiner, reprinted from *Lifelines* (Town House & Country House). Extract from *Women of Jamaica* and 'Into Your Hands' by Jenny Hewer from *Women of Prayer* compiled by Dorothy M. Stewart © Lion Publishing plc Sandy Lane West. Oxford. 'Come Lord Jesus (Morning Prayer)' © Redemptorist Publications. 'A Return to Love' by Marianne Williamson.

A catalogue record for this book is available from the British Library.

Every effort has been made to trace copyright holders. The publishers apologise for any errors or omissions in the above list and would be grateful to be notified of any corrections that should be incorporated into future editions.

Designed by Bill Bolger
Photographs scanned by Les McLean
Printed in the Republic of Ireland by Betaprint. Ltd, Dublin

Veritas books are printed on paper made from the wood pulp of managed forests. For every tree felled, at least one tree is planted, thereby renewing natural resources.

ITEMS SHOULD BE RETURNED ON OR BEFORE THE LAST DATE
SHOWN BELOW. ITEMS NOT ALREADY REQUESTED BY OTHER
READERS MAY BE RENEWED BY PERSONAL APPLICATION, BY
WRITING, OR BY TELEPHONE. TO RENEW, <u>GIVE THE DATE DUE
AND THE NUMBER ON THE BARCODE LABEL.</u>
FINES CHARGED FOR OVERDUE ITEMS WILL INCLUDE POSTAGE
INCURRED IN RECOVERY. DAMAGE TO, OR LOSS OF ITEMS
WILL BE CHARGED TO THE BORROWER.

Leabharlanna Poiblí Chathair Bhaile Átha Cliath
Dublin City Public Libraries

**Dublin City**
Baile Átha Cliath

| Date Due | Date Due | Date Due |
|----------|----------|----------|
| 18. SEP  | RETURN TO BACKSTOCK | |
| 08. | | |

# LOUGH DERG *Simon Kennedy*

A basilica drapes the Island like a hood.
Barefoot pilgrim meander
Over your hobble stones
Of penitential beds.
St Patrick – Pray for us.
St Brigid – Pray for us.
Black tea and toast
Black toast and tea
Sinner save your soul
Toss and turn toward the sea.
Fumble into the dark night
Weary vigil keep
St Brendan – Pray for us.
St Molaise – Pray for us.
European bishop and potentate
Did penance here.
St Patrick saw demons in a cave
Shown to him by God
The afters of the cravings of a guilty hooded mind.
Where pay-as-you-earn taxpayers
Heal their ailing lives
Wincing out the nicotine
In the embrocation of a well bruised sole,
Son of man – Have mercy on me.
The Stationbeds leave bunions and corns in fligits.
The monotonous silence transcends.
The mist falls with real dark grime.
Retreat begins within
'I believe'.

I WOULD LIKE TO THANK the many people who were so generous with their help and stories about Lough Derg especially Monsignor Richard Mohan Prior of Lough Derg, the staff in the office there, Anne Cassidy of Enniskillen for the use of her superb visual interpretations of Lough Derg, and also the huge variety of inspirational pilgrims I met on the island. I think I would also like to thank those who persuaded me that to do the book properly I would have to do the pilgrimage! I did look back when leaving the island. It is a very special place.

Thanks to Helen Carr, my editor in Veritas, who has now mentally done Lough Derg and I'm sure will take her shoes off eventually.

To my constant helpers, especially Paul, thank you for being my companions on the daily journey.

Eileen Good

# Contents

# Foreword

My earliest memories of Lough Derg are of my mother returning from pilgrimage on an afternoon in summertime, often with Lough Derg Rock for us children. I recall her walking the last few miles from the bus and coming into the hayfield where she joined my father and the rest of us to help with the hay.

My own first pilgrimage was made in 1961 along with classmates from school. I made it again the following year and several times during my college years. In 1974 I joined the team of priests working with pilgrims and have been privileged to be part of that team ever since. As student, as priest, as pilgrim, I have been challenged by the pilgrimage. I have often pondered on its meaning and relevance. It is a complex experience, which does not admit of a simple explanation.

Through the years, even centuries, many have tried to say what it means to them. I am very happy that Eileen Good now offers her reflections on this hallowed place and its ancient pilgrimage. Using her own experience of being a pilgrim, along with scripture, poetry and prose, she embraces the complexity of the pilgrim journey. The parallels she draws with the passion, death and Resurrection of our Lord are no accident: our Lough Derg journey is synonymous with the pilgrim journey of Jesus and of life itself.

I know that this book will be welcomed by many who love Lough Derg; it will inspire pilgrims and hopefully give a taste of the spirituality of the pilgrimage to others. I am pleased too that Anne Cassidy's excellent photography, which captures the true spirit of Lough Derg, is given this opportunity to reach a wider audience.

Richard Mohan, Prior
24th June 2003
Feast of the Birth of John the Baptist

# Introduction

To 'do' Lough Derg is to form links with centuries of pilgrims who have come to Lough Derg exploring the issues that surface for every pilgrim in every age. Lough Derg has continued unabated through hardship and oppression and still reaches out today with a call to come apart, take time – and return home renewed and refreshed.

Lough Derg is literally a place apart. Situated in County Donegal, Station Island, also known as St Patrick's Purgatory, is one of about twenty islands on the lake. It is a small island of approximately two acres. St Patrick's association with Lough Derg goes back to the earliest records and since the twelfth century legend has firmly established him there.

For thousands of years pilgrims have 'done' Lough Derg. Its survival to the present day can be described as a mystery, a miracle, a need, a challenge – all of these things – but most of all it is a place of pilgrimage. Accessible only by boat, the island is still a testing ground, where pilgrims undertake a complex pattern of pilgrimage practices which have made no concession to modern living.

Traditionally associated with bare feet and fasting, the entire pilgrimage is much greater than just popular headlines. The penitential practices undertaken make sense in hindsight – they are the pilgrimage, the challenge, the reparation, the lead up to the final morning – the third day – a true resurrection experience. Fasting begins from the midnight before commencing the pilgrimage, and continues until midnight on day three. There is a 'Lough Derg Meal' permitted once on each of the three days when black tea or coffee, dry bread, toast or oatcakes are available.

On arrival on the island, everyone removes their shoes and socks – bare feet are the dress code, and everyone immediately bonds in enduring the hardship of sharp stones and hidden surprises in muddy rock pools. Clothing is dictated by the vagaries of the weather – warm and comfortable for the vigil, guaranteed waterproof for the regular blustery squalls, with pockets to hold the replenishments of insect repellent needed to ward off the midges that aim to remind the pilgrim constantly that this is a pilgrimage, not a holiday.

Nine stations are completed over three days. Each station, involving the constant repetition of familiar prayers around the remains of monastic cells – the penitential beds, located near the Basilica at the water's edge – moves the pilgrim into 'pilgrimage mode'.

The vigil time is both the highlight and the challenge of the three days. Lack of sleep almost numbs the brain. The litany of repetitive prayers eventually becomes a mantra that forms part of the slowing down process and demands a concentration that removes day to day distractions. The sense of being in a place apart is compounded by the isolation, and the bleakness of the location. Although just a short distance from the mainland, the boat journey across adds to the sense of journeying to a place apart. This is time alone, time to examine the realities of daily living, to seek a deeper relationship with self, community and God, in a space and a place tried and tested by pilgrims since the sixth century.

Father I abandon myself into your hands
Do with me what you will.
Whatever you may do, I thank you.
I am ready for all, I accept all.
Let your will be done in me, and in all your creatures.
I wish no more than this O Lord.
Into your hands I commend my spirit.
I offer you all the love of my heart,
For I love you Lord, and I give myself,
Surrender myself into your hands without reserve,
With boundless confidence, for you are my Father.

Charles De Foucauld – 'Prayer of Abandonment'

*Bless to us, O God,*

*The earth beneath our feet.*

*Bless to us, O God,*

*The path whereon we go.*

*Bless to us, O God,*

*The people whom we meet.*

*Amen.*

The Iona Community Worship Book

# The Pilgrims' Place

Lough Derg is challenging and disturbing. The disturbance starts long before you ever set foot on the island – questions surface and won't go away. Will I go? Why should I go? Why am I thinking about Lough Derg now? Could it possibly be as bad as they say? Could I do it? Disturbing questions because they can only be answered by engaging in the experience – which is the challenge.

Planned journeys to specific destinations are exciting, invigorating events. The decision to travel involves planning the route, careful preparations for a safe passage and arrival, coupled with the expectation of a new and stimulating experience. Journeys always offer new possibilities, perhaps even a life-changing experience – who will you meet, what will you see and discover and what will it all mean when you return home. The possibilities are endless.

We are all familiar with Biblical travel stories. The Exodus story, the Christmas Journey of Mary and Joseph, the Three Wise Men, Mary travelling to Elizabeth, Jesus' journey to Calvary, His meeting with two companions on the road to Emmaus – journeys and stories that have all made a difference, and will continue to influence our lives.

Today we are familiar with accounts of great journeys of discovery in our own time – round the world sailing trips, exploring the furthest regions of the planet, travel to outer space, even a moon landing. All life-changing experiences, not just for the travellers, but also for those who benefit from the travels and discoveries. Literature, epic poems, drama, films and television that inspire and challenge are all based on great stories as we participate in the travellers' experience.

Pilgrims have been making the journey to Lough Derg for centuries. Journeys with spiritual 'exploration' can be more difficult both to plan and to execute. The decision to go on pilgrimage necessitates preparations not usually associated with 'taking a break'. The priorities are different. The expectations are different. Socialising, food, fun and shopping are replaced by solitude, fasting, prayer and de-cluttering of self. Fellow travellers on pilgrimage are not chosen, but, like the Emmaus friends, become companions on the journey. Sharing their stories, company, help and support confirm that there are no strangers on this journey, just other pilgrims. The prayers, the vigil, the fasting, the exhaustion, the pain, the support offered, and taken, make it unlike any other time away. Lighting a candle, raising your voice in responses or song, holding the medal or rosary to bring home as tangible evidence of the time apart, confirm a commitment made in the hope of change. This is pilgrimage – travelling in response to a call to repent and pray in a sacred place.

> In the depth of silence
> No words are needed,
> No language required.
> In the depth of silence
> I am called to listen ...
>
> Listen to the beating of your heart.
> Listen to the blowing of the wind,
> The movement of the Spirit.
> Be silent – said the Lord
> And know that I am God.

And listen to the cry of the voiceless.
Listen to the groaning of the hungry.
Listen to the pain of the landless.
Listen to the sight of the oppressed
And to the laughter of children

For that is authentic communication;
Listening to people
Living with people
Dying for people.

Anonymous Indonesian author – 'In the Depths of Silence'

As early as the twelfth century continental pilgrims made their way to Lough Derg, enduring great hardships to travel to a place which they believed held the answer to many of their questions about the afterlife. St Patrick's Purgatory – could our national Saint have known this place?

As with all journey stories, Patrick's begins in a particular
Time and place, that is, with his captivity in the early fifth century. ... In keeping with the classical journey-stories, Patrick conveys more than the outer events; he explores the mystery of life itself, its relationships, its paths to self-knowledge and wisdom, its purpose and meaning, its final goal. Through all life's vicissitudes Patrick has his eyes constantly fixed on Jesus, who journeyed with his disciples through the Holy Land preaching and proclaiming the Good News of the Kingdom of God. The journey of Patrick's Discipleship was a journey of conversion, of

openness to the healing power of Jesus.

Maire B. de Páor – *Patrick – The Pilgrim Apostle of Ireland*

Pilgrim successors to Patrick from Continental Europe, plus the many Irish pilgrims, must have stood together on the mainland at the edge of the grey water, stared across at the unknown and asked the exact same question as pilgrims today – Why am I here? Remember those pilgrims.

Listen to the sounds of history – the wind on the lake, bird song, the hypnotic lapping water, silence. Sounds of foreverness, unscripted, not composed or arranged yet harmonious and blending, sounds of joy and sadness, matins and vespers echoing down the ages.

> Across the hills stand ancient stones
> That cast their songs from times unknown,
> They join the wind through weathered walls
> That held the chant of cloistered halls.

Tom Renaud – 'Soul of Ireland'

Look at the hills, spend some time contemplating them. Round, humped, arched, spreading down to the rocky boggy ground – changing colours, light green, pale green, bright green, brown green, dark green, ever changing artwork repeating the performance for hundreds and hundreds of years. Feel connected to the permanence surrounding you. It is so quiet, so alone, so outside the world and yet it is so brim full with life – which is reality? Is it the world we have temporarily left, or this place which our ancestors thought was at the edge of

their world? Nothing changes. New pilgrims bring perennial questions to a place where answers and decisions are shaped through the reassurance of being in a place which has stood the test of time and pilgrims prayers.

> The gift of prayer
> Is a gift for life,
> For knowing the presence of God
> In times good and bad,
> For knowing the peace of God
> Every year of life,
> And knowing the nearness of God
> When there is worry and anxiety.
> And prayer is the invitation
> And the challenge
> To know the needs of others,
> And to be united with everyone,
> In heaven and earth,
> In the love and life of God.
> Lord, make me truly grateful
> That your gift of prayer
> Is a rock and foundation of my life.
>
> Donal Neary S.J. – *A Lenten Journey*

Lough Derg is one of Europe's most famous places of pilgrimage and has been receiving pilgrims continuously for over a thousand years. A remarkable claim. Who were those people so long ago? Did they really feel the need to take time out, to search for answers all those centuries ago?

In our third millennium, hi-tech world we can be coerced into believing that it is only at this moment in time that problems, worries, and constant questions surface and make us yearn to spend some time in a place apart. Yet in the fifth entury, monks already living an austere and pilgrim life, felt the need to go to a remote place to spend time in prayer and fasting. Searching for answers, the perennial quest. Perhaps like St Augustine, the connection can be to acknowledge that:

> You have made us for yourself and our hearts are restless until they find their rest in you.
>
> *Confessions*

St Davog, supposedly a disciple of St Patrick, was the first abbot of the monastery on Saints Island, approximately one mile from Station Island. Today one of the penitential beds on the Island bears his name, a permanent link with those ancient times. From about the twelfth century, the smaller island or Station Island, St Patrick's Purgatory, today's place of pilgrimage, was sufficiently established as a place of pilgrimage to feature on several medieval maps of Ireland.

The many colourful stories associated with Lough Derg throughout the centuries start with varied accounts of how it first came to be known as Lough 'Derg'. Extraordinary legends relating to the underground cave or cavern situated on Station Island, which was closed in 1780, could have given rise to the use of the Gaelic word *'deirc'* meaning 'eye' or 'opening'. Other reasons for its name concern the Lough itself and St Patrick. Though there is no solid evidence that Patrick ever actually lived on the island, there is a belief that he probably travelled to this remote area in search of peace, tranquillity and, most likely, answers to the many difficult questions that must have surfaced in his mind. During the Middle Ages there were several accounts of St Patrick slaying a monster, perhaps one of the many serpents he encountered, whose blood turned the lake-water red ('*dearg*'). Locals believe that the waters from the surrounding bogland are responsible for the russet tint of the lake.

For whatever reason, the name Lough Derg has been recorded and connected with St Patrick as far back as available records and with this unchallenged tradition of association, the spirituality of our national saint is remembered and renewed annually by the thousands of pilgrims who implore his inspiration and protection.

> I arise today
> Through the strength of heaven;
> Light of sun,
> Radiance of moon,
> Splendour of fire,
> Speed of lighting,
> Swiftness of wind,
> Depth of sea,
> Stability of earth,
> Firmness of rock.

I arise today
Through God's strength to pilot me:
God's eye to look before me,
God's wisdom to guide me,
God's way to lie before me,
God's shield to protect me,
From all who shall wish me ill
Afar and anear,
Alone and in a multitude.
Against every cruel merciless power that may oppose my body and
Soul

– 'St Patrick's Breastplate'

Seeking help 'Against every cruel merciless power that may oppose my body and Soul' may well have been a profound and heartfelt personal prayer by Patrick after he had been granted a first hand glimpse of the torments which awaited those who entered the island's cave or cavern, subsequently known as St Patrick's Purgatory. Patrick's perseverance and commitment to his mission among the Irish was constantly challenged. According to legend, the people refused to change their ways and believe his message of love and conversion to the Gospels, unless the consequences could be authenticated. To find a way forward Patrick became a pilgrim. He took himself to a remote place and undertook a period of prayer, vigil and fasting. At that moment the connection with our most illustrious national saint and today's pilgrims on Lough Derg was established. His prayers were answered.

An account in the *Tractatus de Purgatorio Sancti Patricii* (Treatise on St Patrick's Purgatory) written in 1184 by a monk in the abbey of Saltrey in Huntingdonshire in England reported that Christ himself appeared to Patrick, presented him with a staff and a book of the Gospels and proceeded to give him a detailed account of the horrors awaiting those who entered the cave – purgatory on earth.

> So the Lord took Patrick to a deserted place. There he showed to him a round pit, dark inside, and said to him that whoever, being truly repentant and armed with true faith, would enter this pit and remain for the duration of one day and one night, would be purged of all the sins of his life. Moreover, while going through it, he would see not only the torments of the wicked, but also, if he acted constantly according to the faith, the joys of the blessed.

This description of what would happen to those who ventured into the cave was an inducement to one pilgrim – a knight called Owein – who wanted to further atone for his sins. The stories of the happenings in the cave were sufficiently terrifying for him to need a bishop's permission to enter there. Darkness, fire, demons, torture – all assaulted Owein, and only when he called the name of Jesus did the demons release him. Having survived these ordeals nine times, he then glimpsed the heavenly rewards available and returned to relate his story. In today's world of imaginative marketing, pilgrims can well understand how such an account would be an immediate attraction for intending travellers who wished to avail of first-hand proof of the existence of purgatory. Owein's account of his time of detention in the cave became the basis of many other similarly explicit stories at that time.

Lough Derg, St Patrick's Purgatory in Donegal,
Christendom's purge. Heretial
Around the edges: the centre's hard
As the commensense of a flamboyant bard.
The twentieth century blows across it now
But deeply it has kept an ancient vow.

Patrick Kavanagh – *Lough Derg*

Many centuries later through the most unstable and often violent times, Lough Derg was sustained by the Augustinians and Franciscians and in 1763 a small church, built on the island by the Franciscians, was dedicated to Blessed Virgin Mary of the Angels. The celebrated cave was closed in 1780 and a second church, dedicated to St Patrick, was opened. The present Basilica replaced St Patrick's church, while the present St Mary's Church dates from 1870. From that time to the present day the development of Lough Derg as a place of pilgrimage, in the tradition of St Patrick, has continued unabated.

The constant upgrading of accommodation and the construction of new buildings necessitated reclaiming land from the lake to augment the original island site of one acre. The construction of the church from 1926-1930 was a major undertaking at that time. It opened on 1 June 1931 and was subsequently honoured with the title 'Basilica' by Pope Pius XI.

It is worth reflecting, in our world of technology and accessible comfortable travel, on the centuries of pilgrims who travelled to Lough Derg. Despite

unspeakable hardships, plus fines and penalties likely to be imposed on them for participating, they travelled, brought family and friends and went home renewed. It is perhaps the great mystery of Lough Derg, where the only 'appeal' is hardship and penance that pilgrims continue to travel there to renew their faith. The first-time pilgrims face the three days with hope, prayer and a certain apprehension, while regular pilgrims, despite knowing the challenges, undertake the journey each year. All reasons for 'doing' Lough Derg are valid. There is no material gain, no public acknowledgement of having endured the hardship and pain – it is between the pilgrim and God why they chose to be there.

> I see a girl climbing the mountain
> In a red blouse and blue jeans
> Rolled up to the middle of her shinbones,
> No shoes on her feet meeting the sharp stones,
> Climbing among rocks, a smile on her face
> Though her mind may be bleeding from old
> And new wounds. In time, she accosts the saint
> And in the silence a story is told,
> A drop is added to the deepening sea
> At the top of the mountain before she
> Faces down to the world from that brief height.
> Below her, for miles around, the fields
> Are graves for sheep that never saw the Spring light
> In grass kneeling to receive the bones and skulls.
>
> Brendan Kennelly – 'The Pilgrim'

Young and old, all who are physically able to participate in the rituals and fasting, make each group of pilgrims a miniature cross-section of the human race. Who are they? Why have they come? What are their prayers?

> Health, jobs,
> health, love,
> health, hope
> courage, friendship,
> peace of mind, decisions,
> Faith, belief,
> Thank you God for all your goodness.

The teenagers studying for examinations, making career choices, begging for help, parents pleading for them and for themselves – the sick, the lonely, the confused, the depressed, the relieved, the happy, young and old – all connected through bare feet, prayer, fasting, forgiveness and thanksgiving.

Prayers of thanksgiving soar to the heavens – thanksgiving for 'God's goodness' – a different definition to each person, and a concluding part of each petition. In the ritual of Lough Derg, there is a plan that allows the community of pilgrims to unite as searching people in a sacred place. The variety of men and women who make Lough Derg a penitential destination represents all humankind praying for guidance, inspiration and courage.

Lord, make me know your ways.
Lord, teach me your paths.
Make me walk in your truth, and teach me:
For you are God my saviour.

Remember your mercy, Lord,
And the love you have shown from of old.
In your love remember me,
Because of your goodness, O Lord.

The Lord is good and upright.
He shows the path to those who stray,
He guides the humble in the right path;
He teaches his way to the poor.

  Psalm 24

*Lord make us the prophets of our times,*
*Pilgrims not wayfarers.*
*May each day begin*
*With prayerful preparation*
*Opening our hearts*
*To a spirit of loving repentance.*
*Make us aware, that although individuals,*
*We travel with others*
*And help us to keep vigil with you*
*In that holy place within the heart.*
*May each event and meeting of the day*
*Be Eucharist*
*Leaving behind something of ourselves*
*In Sacrifice*
*So that we can celebrate and exult with joy,*
*Determined to allow Christ*
*Be reflected in us more and more*
*Thus heralding a new age*
*Of hope and joy and freedom.*
*Amen.*

'The Pilgrim Prayer'

# Starting Out

To leave the trappings of todays' instant technological communications for a desert experience is to seek solitude with a graced trust. Taking time to journey to a place apart, a remote place, totally dependent on self, hoping to find answers, peace of heart, of mind, demands courage, faith and prayer.

In a gesture instantly synonymous with dependency and hardship, and in solidarity with the poorest, pilgrims take off their shoes. In that gesture they remove a symbolic connection with daily living and prepare to travel the road 'having taken nothing for the journey'. Bare feet. Sore feet. There is no escape. Big stones hurt, small stones hurt. Every stone is a reminder of penance – as valid a part of the Lough Derg experience as the fasting and prayers.

Starting the pilgrimage barefooted links the pilgrim with the first night of the Easter Triduum when the disciples removed their sandals and Jesus washed their feet, the beginning of three days that culminated in the joy of Resurrection.

In Lough Derg, centuries of prayers resonate in the air. It is a holy place. To pray in solitude, developing a commitment to regular contact with God can provide the pilgrim with a precious, everlasting souvenir of time spent apart from the daily merry-go-round of modern living. Sharing this relationship is essential to the community of pilgrims praying as a body to a compassionate, listening God. Prayer-time on Lough Derg is total immersion in heartfelt intercessions – familiar prayers of petition and thanksgiving, a mantra of loved and trusted phrases.

Sacred Heart of Jesus I place all my trust in Thee

Jesus Mercy, Mary Help.

The Rosary
Hail Mary Full of Grace
The Lord is with Thee
Blessed art Thou Amongst Women
And Blessed is the Fruit of Thy Womb, Jesus
Holy Mary, Mother of God
Pray for us sinners
Now and at the hour of our death.
Amen.

Hours of repetition of the familiar and loved begin to make sense of the pain. Everything becomes crystal clear, senses are heightened – all the suffering becomes the prayer. The fasting, the exhaustion, and the sore feet infuse the words with an urgency that demands a response. Moving around the Basilica, inside and out, surrounded by a community of searching, praying companions, evokes a timeless continuity in an ancient place. It is a Celtic Christian ritual that comforts by its permanence.

In the widest sense, Christian prayer is a personal response to the felt presence of God in an effort to intensify that presence as a significant force in human existence.

*The New Dictionary of Theology*

The pattern of the pilgrimage days ahead is clearly outlined. The boat journey to the island immediately draws the mind away from the daily routine onto the challenge of three unique days.

Fasting begins the midnight before arriving and continues until the midnight after leaving the island. Shoes and socks are removed in the dormitory before going to the Basilica to begin the First Station. Nine Stations are completed over three days. One Lough Derg meal is allowed each day. The vigil – the central penitential exercise of the pilgrimage – involves staying completely and continuously awake for twenty-four hours. It commences at 10 pm on day one, and continues until 10 pm on day two.

The Stations begin with a visit to the Blessed Sacrament in St Patrick's Basilica. This first ritual allows the pilgrim to spend time contemplating the task ahead and to ask for the graces and blessings needed to undertake the pilgrimage. Some will use the days ahead as time to do penance, for others it will be a chance to review and reflect, and for many it will be an opportunity to give thanks in the most physical way possible – enduring discomforts totally alien to a modern, comfort-driven world. The communal prayer for all will be for courage, not just to stay the pilgrimage, but life's journey.

> Come to me, all you who labour and are overburdened, and I will give you rest. Shoulder my yoke and learn from me, for I am gentle and humble in heart, and you will find rest for your Souls. Yes, my yoke is easy and my burden light.
>
> Matthew 11:28-30

To surrender to an invitation to participate with confidence, is an immediate response to prayer. The first moments of the pilgrimage are possibly the most difficult and yet the most exciting. This is both journey's end and beginning. It can be daunting to think of the days ahead, planned in every detail by those who hope to provide a map of recovery for the weary traveller.

To pray in the company of hundreds of pilgrim companions, all praying in faith and hope, inspires confidence that the prayers will be answered.

> There is no need to worry; but if there is anything you need pray for it, asking God for it with prayer and thanksgiving, and that peace of God, which is so much greater than we can understand, will guard your hearts and your thoughts, in Christ Jesus.
>
> Philippians 4:6-9

Throughout the journey are rituals to focus the restless mind. This moment in the Basilica is with the waiting God who asks nothing more than your presence, your company. This silent mutual greeting is the first prayer.

> Faith is a decision to enter into a personal relationship with God surrender to God ...{it is}... an act of the whole person involving intellect and will as well as emotions and feelings.
> – *The Experience of God – An Invitation to Do Theology*
>
> Dermot A. Lane

The ritual of prayer on the island forms the foundation of the pilgrimage.

The intensity of the communal prayer bonds the pilgrims. The concentration evident in those participating helps the weary and, eventually, the raised voices orchestrate a harmonious chorus of united prayers. The prayers of centuries linger and encourage

Communal prayer on Lough Derg is held in the Basilica. An enormous building, it dominates the island, offering shelter and sanctuary to all. As a successor to the infamous cave of unspeakable torment and the subsequent 'Prison Chapel', the present Basilica is the shelter for the vigil, far removed from the terrors endured centuries earlier. One of the leading architects of the time, Professor W.A. Scott designed the building in 1919, shortly after he visited the island. Because of the unsettled political times in Ireland he was unable to commence building. Professor Scott died in 1921 and the building began under T.J. Cullen and continued during the years 1926-1931. As intended by Professor Scott, the austere octagonal dome is clearly visible from the mainland. It is truly an awesome sight to behold, in the context of the size of the site available for the construction of such a building. The building took four years to complete at a cost of £80,000 and was designated a Basilica in 1931.

The size of the Basilica, with its rugged solid exterior, suggests safety and sanctuary for all who venture in. As befits the Lough Derg pilgrimage, the interior design is plain, functional and provides a simple yet spacious background for the rituals and liturgies of the pilgrimage programme. There are two striking images in the Basilica, the wooden cross and the Stations of the Cross; both are sources of light, both are connected through the Cross.

The enormous wooden cross at the back of the sanctuary, based on a penal cross and designed by the eminent sculptor Imogen Stuart, has an opening in the wood around the head of the figure. Symbolically, the use of an opening to let in light over the suffering Jesus is a powerful symbol of hope and resurrection. The other wonderful source of light and colour is through each of the stained-glass windows. Designed by the celebrated Dublin artist, Harry Clarke, each window represents a Station of the Cross. Within each window, Our Lady, St Paul and each of the twelve Apostles are shown holding one of the moments of the Lord's last journey. As with all of Harry Clarke's work, the use of colour and the design of the images lift the eyes and heart upwards even on the dullest of Lough Derg days. When the western sun shines through making the stunning colours glow, each window tells its story with a new meaning.

> People are like stained-glass windows. They sparkle and shine when the sun is out, but when the darkness sets in, their true beauty is revealed only if there is light from within.
>
> Elizabeth Kübler-Ross

The story of the Passion, Death and Resurrection – the three dark days – echoes through the Lough Derg days. Being alone, in pain and suffering, receiving help and encouragement, praying, the tomb experience, the conclusion and then returning, renewed in mind and body.

*Lord, thank you that you are a pilgrim God;*

*a God who continually goes out on Pilgrimage in*

*order to bring your people to the place*

*of promise,*

*of fulfilment,*

*of home.*

Ruth Patterson
*– Journeying Towards Reconciliation: A Song for Ireland*

# Moving On

The exterior starting point for the station brings the pilgrim immediately back to Patrick – kneeling at St Patrick's Cross near the Basilica, where the first Our Fathers, Hail Marys and Creeds are recited. The ornamental plinth holding the cross is the oldest surviving relic on the island, dating back to about the ninth century.

In his book *Patrick In His Own Words*, Bishop Joseph Duffy talks of how Patrick related to God:

> Patrick's God was of primary importance to him. He was not a distant and disapproving God but rather loving and accepting. The partnership between them created a dynamic harmony. Patrick accepted God's love with total trust, but he also felt accountable to God for all his actions. His concern was to do what was right rather than what he wanted for himself.

Pilgrimage prayers on Lough Derg have had a defined pattern of continuity since the 1600s when a Franciscian friar, Brother Michael O'Cleary, detailed the prayers to be said, the exercises to be performed, and named the saints to be associated with each of the penitential beds. These beds, an important part of each station, are the remains of beehive cells from early monastic times. Brother O'Cleary also named the saints to be associated with each of the penitential beds – Saints Brigid, Brendan, Catherine, Columba or Columcille, Patrick, and the last bed was dedicated to two local abbots, St Davog the local patron of Lough Derg, and St Molaise of Devenish. St Davog is also remembered on the mainland, where on the top of one of the mountains near the ferry St Davog's Chair offers a spectacular view of the

islands. The only non-Irish saint associated with the beds is St Catherine of Alexandria, who was martyred in the fourth century.

This ritual of penitential prayer was confirmed by a Dominican, Dominic O'Brollaghan, in 1735 and is in daily use today since the first issue of the present pilgrims's leaflet in 1876. A further connection with pilgrims past and present.

Traditionally, pilgrims stand and kiss St Patrick's Cross before moving to St Brigid's Cross on the wall of the Basilica. This cross dates from about the twelfth century and was originally on the wall of the old St Patrick's Church. Kneeling at the Cross, the pilgrim recites three Our Fathers, three Hail Marys and the Creed. Then each pilgrim, standing with his back to the cross, arms outstretched in the shape of the cross, says three times: 'I renounce the world, the flesh and the devil' – publicly rejecting all that prevents him from following the way of truth and love.

> Beside St Brigid's Cross – an ancient relic
> A fragment of the Middle Ages set
> Into the modern masonry of the conventional Basilica
> Where everything is ordered and correct –
> A queue of pilgrims waiting to renounce
> The World, the Flesh, the Devil and all his house.
>
> Patrick Kavanagh – *Lough Derg*

From there the pilgrim commences the ritual of walking four times around the Basilica while reciting seven decades of the Rosary and the Creed. At this early stage of the pilgrimage, the need to stay focused on the prayers, the words, and intentions becomes vital in order not to focus on jagged stones and bruised feet.

The next stage is to move on to praying at the penitential beds. Doing the rounds, saying the order of prayers, holding the usually sodden leaflet of instructions – all combine to make the brain shout 'Penance! This is penance!' Could this be the reason I am here? Why am I here? I am here because I choose to be here. I want to succeed, I am able for this challenge. Three days – the whole triduum encompasses the Passion, Death and Resurrection.

The six penitential beds present a constant challenge to the pilgrim. Six circles of stone, the remains of monastic cells of the ninth century, they look as forbidding and unforgiving as they are. Relics of an era of penance and austerity, time has merely sharpened their existence lest pilgrims expect any concessions to present day comforts.

> The middle of the island looked like the memory
> Of some village evicted by the Famine,
> Some corner of a field beside a well
> Old stumps of walls where a stunted boortree is growing
> These were the hold cells of saintly men –
>
> Patrick Kavanagh – *Lough Derg*

Three times around the outside of each bed while saying three Our Fathers, three Hail Marys and the Creed, all repeated while kneeling at the entrance to each bed, and again while negotiating around the inside of the circle of stones – culminating in praying at the cross at the centre of the bed. The cross, with the figure of the Crucified Christ, is at the centre of each bed. The worn figure shines with the weight of petitions as each pilgrim sub-consciously leans on the cross for support, as they try to straighten up and continue the journey.

> Lord, Simon met with you in a way he had never expected. At times we too can suddenly be faced with someone in need of our help. May we not turn away, but willingly offer whatever help we can give.
>
> *Way of the Cross* – 5th Station

Every step, every stumble, every prayer is penance. Every fall is a reminder of The Passion – Jesus fell three times.

> Lord, we know that you walk with us each day we face the cares and challenges of life. Help us to keep going, especially in times of weakness, and to trust in you in times of depression and despair.
>
> *Way of the Cross* – 9th Station

Each hand stretched out to help, to steady a fall, every look or smile that encourages is prayer in action. This is pilgrimage. All on the same journey, compassionate, caring, encouraging.

Veronica saw your face, Lord, and your face left an impression. Your face is the face of suffering and need, the face of the aged, of the undernourished child, of the refugee. Your face today is around us if only we look. 'I was sick and you visited me, naked and you clothed me.'

*Way of the Cross* – 6th Station

Walking around the beds, kneeling at the entrance, walking around the interior, all the time in bare feet, is the most physical prayer. The entire body, all the senses, are alert to each moment. Every stone is a hazard, every pool of water holds hidden shocks – wet mud, instead of being avoided, becomes a soft cushion to ease the pain. Concentration on the moment is the only way forward – why am I here? God Almighty, hear my prayer. Promises are visibly made – hardships 'offered up' for petitions worthy of Lough Derg's penance.

> For family – guard us, protect us
> For health – heal us
> For love – show us
> For decisions – inspire us
> For forgiveness – grant us
> For courage – give us
> For faith – help us
> From addictions – cure us
> In old age – guide us
> In death – receive us

When all the beds have been negotiated the pilgrim then goes to the water's edge. Lough Derg is an island – water is a powerful symbol – both a connection to and separation from the mainland. The journey over by boat physically puts space between daily living and the place apart. This is the stretch of water that, once in the history of the pilgrimage, claimed the lives of ninety pilgrims as they made their way to Lough Derg. On Sunday 12 July 1795 ninety-three people set out to travel to the island. A short distance from the quay the boat started taking water and, despite being close to land, sank in about ten feet of water. Only three people survived the tragedy. Twenty of the victims are buried in a mass grave on Friar's Island. In St Mary's Church a sad reminder of that day is displayed, a small wooden cross dated 1792, which was found in the hand of one of the victims, Miss O'Donnell from Derry.

Standing at the lakeside, looking at the movement of the water – the pilgrim says five Our Fathers, five Hail Marys and the Creed. Pilgrimage ritual at the lake is also a link with the Middle Ages when pilgrims completely immersed themselves in the water.

> The word Baptism is derived from the Greek '*bapto*' meaning 'to dip' or 'to immerse'. Ritual washings were common religious practices in the first century c.e. These were external rites of purification, signifying what they effected – death to an old way of life; rebirth into a new community.
>
> *The New Dictionary of Theology*

Kneeling at the water's edge, the pilgrim repeats the prayers. In previous times, pilgrims walked out into the lake to pray while standing, and then kneeling, on bruising stones. In one of the few references to physical healing on the island, pilgrims could go out to a large smooth rock in the lake known as the 'monks' stone of penance', which supposedly bore the imprint of St Patrick's knees. This stone was believed to bring relief to the pains and aches of the pilgrims' knees and feet.

The pilgrim returns to St Patrick's Cross to pray one Our Father, one Hail Mary and a Creed. The first station is then concluded in the Basilica by saying five Our Fathers, five Hail Marys and the Creed or Psalm 15 for the Pope's intentions.

There are nine of these stations to be completed during the pilgrimage. Three stations are made on the first day, four during the night-time of the vigil, one on the day following the vigil and the ninth on the morning of departure from the island.

*Black tea and toast*

*Black toast and tea*

Simon Kennedy –'Lough Derg'

T he completion of the first full station allows the pilgrim to partake of some food, breaking the fast for the first time. Fasting as part of the pilgrimage ritual commences at midnight before arriving on Lough Derg. In the Gospels we have many examples of Jesus fasting in a place apart.

Then Jesus was led by the Spirit out into the desert to be put to the test by the devil. He fasted for forty days and forty nights, after which he was hungry, and the tester came and said to him, 'If you are Son of God, tell these stones to turn into loaves'. But he replied, 'Scripture says "Human beings live not on bread alone, but on every word that comes from the mouth of God."'

Matthew 4:1-4.

The tradition of fasting on Lough Derg is as old as the pilgrimage itself. The early monastic settlements on the island would have had fasting built into their lives as part of the tradition of living a remote and austere life – a life of penance and repentance. In monastic life today, the practice of fasting, eating only simple food as prescribed by their rule, is part of daily life. Fasting, in order to prepare, is still part of our Christian lives. Fasting before receiving Holy Communion. Fasting on Ash Wednesday and Good Friday.

In the Old Testament the people fasted to ask forgiveness and seek help; in the New Testament Jesus fasted before praying and healing; and in the present day fasting has both the traditional connotation of penance and the modern day symbolism of solidarity with those in our world who are not fasting, but starving. Fasting on pilgrimage can be used as an opportunity for reflection and examination of attitudes in our lives.

The importance of authentic fasting is an integral part of Patrick's spiritual legacy to the Irish, and has been practised by all our great saints through the ages. Though advantageous to health and general well-being, this kind of fasting was primarily focused on God, and was motivated by a desire for conversion of heart. This resulted in the opening up of the penitent's heart to the spiritual and temporal needs of the neighbour, and true fasting was thus linked with almsgiving and prayer:

'Is not this the fast that I choose:
To loose the bonds of injustice, to undo the thongs of the
Yoke,
To let the oppressed go free and to break every yoke?
Is it not to share your bread with the hungry, and bring
the homeless poor into your house;
When you see the naked to cover him, and not to hide yourself from
your own kin?...
Then you shall call and the Lord will answer; You shall cry for help
and he will say, here I am.' (Isaiah 58:6-7, 9)

Maire B. de Paor – *Patrick – the Pilgrim Apostle of Ireland*

Today's Lough Derg meal is far removed from earlier days. Previously during the nine day pilgrimage pilgrims were forbidden any food before, during or after the day of the vigil. The 'Lough Derg Soup' – hot water with pepper and salt – can be regarded as part of the penance or a welcome addition to the menu depending on the requirements of the pilgrims. Mealtime in the Refectory consists of dry toast, oatcakes, black tea or coffee – hot, tasty, and all the more appetising because of the anticipation of waiting. It is food for travellers and pilgrims, basic and sufficient. No milk or butter is allowed. For many today it is no more than they are allowed in various allergy diets, or perhaps what some would choose to have when they detoxify the body rather than the soul.

An important element of the Lough Derg meal is the opportunity for mealtime companionship. Traditionally, monasteries offered hospitality and sanctuary to the pilgrim. In the Gospels we have many examples of Jesus using mealtimes to talk to people, to perform miracles and generally to enjoy their company. At the Wedding Feast of Cana he performed his first miracle; when he saw that the five thousand followers who had gone apart to listen to him were hungry, he fed them; and it was at mealtime during the Last Supper that he gave us Everlasting Food.

Shared mealtime in Lough Derg is a time for sharing stories and getting the encouragement of those who also abstain in a similar spirit of penance and hope. It's a time to listen to the mixture of accents. Every county seems represented. Where are you from? Football and hurling. Listening to the stories. Have you been here before? How are the feet? Look out for the midges, the slippery rocks around the beds, the sharp rocks in the pools of water. The workers, the unemployed, the professionals, the clergy, the mothers who come every year, the parents on pilgrimage together, grieving for a child cruelly taken by the modern tragedy of drugs and depression, all seem to raise a smile as they bond and share hospitality in the time-honoured tradition of pilgrims always and everywhere.

*I said to the man who stood at the gate of the Year,*

*'Give me a light that I may tread safely into the*

*unknown.' And he replied,*

*'Go out into the darkness and put your hand into the*

*hand of God. That shall be to you better than light*

*and safer than a known way.'*

Minnie Louise Haskins (1875-1957)
(Quoted by King George VI in his Christmas broadcast 25
December 1939)

> He came back to the disciples and found them sleeping,
> And He said to Peter 'So you had not the strength to keep awake with Me
> one hour?
> You should be awake, and praying not to be put to the
> test. The spirit is willing, but the flesh is weak.'
>
> Mark 14:37

The loneliness, the sense of being forgotten, of feeling abandoned by his friends is palpable in Jesus' words. The loneliness of Gethsemene. The disciples must have been shattered by their inability to stay awake and be supportive. Were they cold and hungry – were they exhausted from praying and waiting – were they asleep on their feet – were they in their bare feet?

Perhaps it is only when one has 'done' Lough Derg, that is it really possible to understand the disciples falling asleep during their vigil. Staying awake demands concentration. To keep vigil with companions in need is to enter into solidarity with them. It is a most caring, compassionate and tangible form of support. Being on a vigil can most often be just that – being there for someone, having someone there for you. Not to feel alone, to know that someone cares, cares enough to stay the journey, is the essence of keeping vigil.

We associate vigil with support needed in a time of crisis – staying by the bedside of a loved one who may not even know we're there, supporting someone who is waiting for or dreading a phone-call – hospital tests, exam results, travellers' safety, waiting, hoping, praying. Holding someone who finds the night intolerable and dreads the morning. Staying with the dying until the parting is final. Being there for the bereaved long after the crowds have departed.

Stay with me,
Remain here with me,
Watch and pray, watch and pray.

   Taizé

Keeping vigil in a sacred place is a central part of pilgrimage. Night approaches. There is a silence of the night. Senses are sharpened and there is an air of expectation, of mystery and waiting.

Nothing can make the night stay outside
It pours in everywhere, smothers my room
With black air prepared in some unseen cave,
Tightens around my skull the root silence
Of that room in rock; nothing broke the dark
Except the tick of raindrops from above;
Centuries seeping through the limestone
To point a cold finger of stalactite
At emptiness never softened by breath;
Where the sore of absence never felt
In cold that fasted solid from light,
A hermit space that let in no question.
This dark is all eyes, but cannot feel
How it blackens the breath and the heart.
It weighs me down as it would a stone.

   John O'Donohue – 'The Night'

Being open to what the night might reveal through contemplation, prayer and communal exercises enables the pilgrim to use the vigil as a gifted opportunity rather than a prescribed exercise to be endured in order to fulfil the requirements of pilgrimage. The rituals of the night, the prayers, the gestures, the stations, the waiting, the cold, the tiredness, all combine to make the vigil a unique and testing experience. Each sensation is part of the total awareness of pilgrimage.

An all night vigil can be a lonely experience, even when surrounded by pilgrim companions. I'm so lonely. Am I the only one? Lonely. The very word drains the heart and numbs hope. The seemingly endless darkness of twenty-four sleepless hours stretches ahead. An unwelcome emotion at any time, in the dark of night loneliness can be a constant companion. Finding the nerve to conquer fear of the unknown, courage to trust in a caring, listening God can bring renewed energy to the journey.

The pilgrims unite in the Basilica, with its connection to previous pilgrims incarcerated in the cave – Purgatory. They unite to find their way through the night hours. Almost immediately the prospect of no sleep becomes the main preoccupation as night commences. This is vigil – this is staying awake and keeping watch – the Gethsemene experience. Three earth-shattering days stretched ahead for Jesus. The Lough Derg vigil is a chosen time connected by prayer, waiting, repentance and Eucharist.

'Doing the Stations' in the Basilica during the vigil confirms the notion of being in the 'cave' – crowds of people in one place praying, doing penance and waiting for the dawn. As the night unfolds, as the cold seeps into every

pore, the longing for sleep becomes almost unbearable. The penance of staying awake touches every nerve in the body. Movement, prayer, ritual all become tools to ward off sleep. Stay awake! Who else in the world is awake through the night? Keep vigil with them – insomniacs, carers, night shift workers, the homeless, the sick, women in labour, the lonely. Remember those who have chosen a life where every night they keep vigil, waiting and praying as the new day dawns. As morning breaks, the night sky is streaked with the faintest glow of light – a new day, a new beginning.

Participating in a communal Rosary in the Basilica, during the night vigil, provides an opportunity for all the pilgrims present to unite in praying the loved and familiar.

> As though the music of the ocean
> Had come to shelter
> On the home hearth
>
> Dreaming of itself
> In the selfsame dream
> From a far distant region
>
> In buoyant ease
> Between the fill and fall
> Of waves of Hail Marys.
>
>   John O'Donohue – 'The Rosary'

To wait in hope for the dawn can be the beginning of the pilgrimage and the move from loneliness to solitude can be the blessing of the vigil.

> In our darkness there is no darkness with you,
> O Lord.
> The deepest night is clear as the daylight.
>
> Taizé

Morning Mass has a tangible air of expectation, celebration of the eagerly awaited new day. Despite the fact that the vigil is not even halfway through there is already a sense of achievement that the night has passed away and the light of day rekindles the spirit. The congregation's involvement in the Mass, the prayers and responses, supported by words of encouragement, provide sustenance for the remainder of the vigil, the remainder of the pilgrimage. It is still at the tomb stage – Resurrection day is not yet here.

> There are no outsiders here: in bare feet, everyone is equal. Pilgrims journey together: they share each other's joy, feel each other's pain. We try to ensure that everyone's story is heard and that help is offered for the continuing journey of life.
>
> *The Lough Derg Pilgrimage Brochure*

Despite the presence of many other pilgrims during a vigil, it is a deeply personal time – time to be alone, but not lonely, time to experience solitude. This solitude can be an opportunity to move into a relationship of prayer, and the prayers of the night can be utterly different to the prayers of the morning.

> I bow my knees before the Father of our Lord Jesus Christ,
> From whom every family in heaven and on earth takes its name.
> I pray that, according to the riches of His glory,
> He may grant that you may be strengthened in your inner being with power through His Spirit,
> And that Christ may dwell in your hearts through faith,
> As you are being rooted and grounded in love.
> I pray that you may have the power to comprehend, with all the saints,
> What is the breadth and length
> And height and depth,
> And to know the love of Christ that surpasses knowledge,
> So that you may be filled with all the fullness of God.
>
> Ephesians 3:14-19

The solitude of the vigil should not become an opportunity to dwell in locked silence on daily hurts and disappointments. The challenge rather is, within the peace and tranquillity of the vigil, to find the courage to reach out and source that most elusive companion – self.

Here I am, O Lord, in search of myself,
That I may find life's meaning and purpose
For me in my age and circumstance,
Lord, show me myself.

Here I am, O Lord, in search of my neighbours
Through their needs, frustrations and hopes,
Lord, show me my neighbours.

Here I am, O Lord in search of You
As I search for myself and my neighbours,
Lord, show me Yourself.

*Women of Jamaica*

The lighting of the vigil candle signifies hope – the light shining in the dark.

I light a candle
And suddenly
The world about me
Changes,
I am reminded
Yet again
That one small flame
Is all it takes
To let the darkness know
It cannot win.

Ruth Patterson – 'I Light A Candle'

The ritual of the vigil is tested and testing. It is the great challenge of Lough Derg. The tradition of keeping watch, praying, waiting for the new dawn, new day.

*Happy those whose offence is forgiven,*
*whose sin is remitted.*
*O happy those to whom the Lord*
*imputes no guilt,*
*in whose spirit is no guile.*

*But now I have acknowledged my sins;*
*my guilt I did not hide.*
*I said: 'I will confess*
*my offence to the Lord.'*
*And you, Lord, have forgiven*
*the guilt of my sin.*

*Rejoice, rejoice in the Lord,*
*exult, you just!*
*O come, ring out your joy,*
*all you upright of heart.*

Psalm 31:1-2, 5-11

# Reconciliation & Renewal

Early stories of the horrors of the visions in the cave confirmed for medieval pilgrims the need to repent and do penance in this world. Lough Derg – St Patrick's Purgatory. 'To go to confession' is still one of the reasons often given by pilgrims for going on pilgrimage.

The Sacrament of Reconciliation takes place at 8.30 am, during the vigil. The earlier hours of darkness and solitude are uninterrupted opportunities for soul searching and reflection. Daily distractions seem remote and unimportant as layer after layer of guilt, pain and fear are revealed and acknowledged. Release from the hurt of emotions, deep and painful, needs the courage to accept the gift of God's forgiveness freely given and available to all.

The situation of Lough Derg, remote and untouched by modern times, peels away the distractions of daily living and connects us with our most basic needs – to repent, to be assured of forgiveness and given an opportunity to try again. During each vigil, hundreds of pilgrims take part in the Sacrament of Reconciliation, and for those who wish to avail of further help there is a counselling service available at any time. The crowds of people, gathered in an atmosphere of forgiveness and healing, are conducive to trusting and believing in the possibility of new beginnings.

Following the hours of solitude and prayer, morning seems an appropriate time for the Sacrament of Reconciliation. A visibly emotional ceremony in an atmosphere of compassion and healing, hundreds of pilgrims fulfill one of the highlights of their pilgrimage as they confess, repent and rejoice in God's unconditional love.

'For here's the day of a poor soul freed
To a marvellous beauty above its head.'

The gift of God's forgiveness comes to the pilgrims, according to
Kavanagh, as an experience of interior liberation from sin and evil and
is construed as something precious conferred on the penitent from a
source which is immeasurably more wonderful than any earthly agent.
... The Christian religion believes that God's love for every single
human being is inexhaustible and unconditional.

Tom Stack – *No Earthly Estate. God and Patrick Kavanagh:
An anthology*

The great tradition of praying for those loved ones gone before us, grieving
for them, including them in Masses offered and in the penances endured, is
a significant part of pilgrims' prayers. It almost seems possible to physically
work the grief out of the body, out of the soul, into the pain of sharp rocks
and stones under bare feet. The belief, that through prayers and penance
here on earth we can intercede for the souls in Purgatory and shorten their
time there, is evidenced by the prayers and actions of the pilgrims.

These departed ones can be aided by the prayers and good works of those
living on earth.

*The New Dictionary of Theology*

Baptism incorporates us into Christ and forms us into God's people. This first sacrament pardons all our sins, rescues us from the power of darkness, and brings us to the dignity of adopted children.

*The New Dictionary of Theology*

A full Basilica resounding with the traditional response 'I do' to the Baptismal questions is a radical reminder of the commitment made for us, many years previously, by devoted faithful followers, during a Station at St Brigid's Cross the pilgrim has an opportunity to recall Baptism when publicly renouncing the world, the flesh and the devil. The symbolism of water and Baptism is evident as each station concludes with prayers at the water's edge

There is time during these hours to remain for a while in the Blessed Sacrament Chapel, where there is an immediate sense of prayerful adoration. Time to reflect on the vigil so far, to think on the hours ahead, time perhaps to remember again the reasons for coming to Lough Derg.

Three o'clock in the afternoon is traditionally the time for praying the Way of the Cross. With the help of the stunning Harry Clarke windows, and their absolutely unique portrayal of each station it is almost possible to say, 'I know how it feels'. Stripped bare of all that normally seems to matter, tired and sore from falling, grateful for all help given, an overwhelming sense of being forgotten, buried in hope – praying for Resurrection.

Is it true that after this life of ours we shall one day be
Awakened
By a terrifying clamour of trumpets?
Forgive me, God, but I console myself
That the beginning and resurrection of all of us dead
Will simply be announced by the crowing of the cock.

After that we'll remain lying down a while ...
The first to get up
Will be Mother ... we'll hear her
Quietly laying the fire,
Quietly putting the kettle on the stove
And cosily taking the teapot out of the cupboard
We'll be home once more.

    Vladimir Holan – 'Resurrection'

The celebration of the Eucharist on the evening of the vigil is a memorable gathering of pilgrims who are 'waiting in joyful hope for the coming of our Saviour Jesus Christ'.

In an atmosphere of reverence and anticipation, the Basilica is filled with a community welcomed around the table of the Lord, singing his praises, united in prayer and nurtured with the Bread of Life. There are no strangers at the meal. The previous hours of preparation, prayer, meditation and reconciliation lead joyfully to this celebration. At this banquet, through the support of those present, petitions and prayers are shared and celebrated

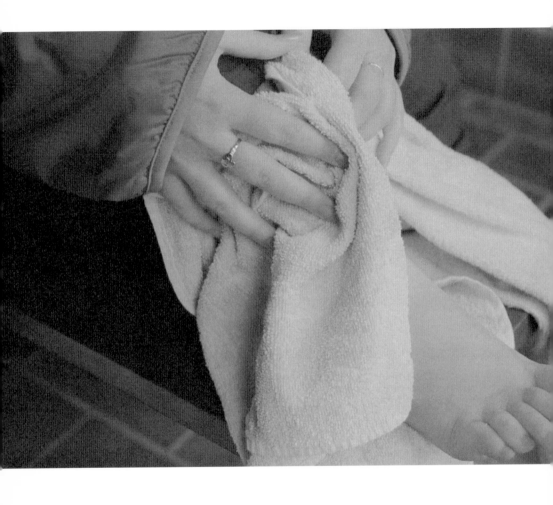

making this Eucharist a memorable experience to carry back to daily life. A reminder of the Meal to be shared always with those we meet on the daily journey of life.

Night prayer, Benediction and the Conclusion of the Vigil fill the remaining hours of staying awake and keeping watch. Darkness falls. All is quiet. Prayers are renewed and a sense of quiet achievement prevails as the crowds empty from the Basilica and make their way to the dormitories. There is a tangible anticipation of sleep. Within minutes of arriving in the dormitory, feet are gently tended. It is no longer forbidden to lie down and stretch out, eyes can now legitimately close and the waves of tiredness can become blessed sleep.

> Father, I place into your hands
> My friends and family.
> Father, I place into your hands
> The things that trouble me,
> Father, I place into your hands
> The person I would be,
> For I know I always can trust you.
>
> Jenny Hewer – 'Into Your Hands'

*God of my life, I welcome this new day,*

*It is your gift to me, a new creation,*

*A promise of resurrection.*


*I thank you for the grace of being alive this morning.*

*I thank you for the sleep that has refreshed me.*

*I thank you for this chance to make a new beginning.*


Come Lord Jesus – Morning Prayer

# New Day, New Beginnings

'On the third day he rose again' – it is the third day – Resurrection Day. At 6.00 am the bell for rising announces the new day, vigil over, last day on Lough Derg.

The closing Mass at 6.30 am is a quiet celebration, a sense of achievement, of being almost there. Reflection after Communion is an opportunity to pray those prayers again, to revisit all those urgent intentions, to give thanks for the graces received and think awhile about returning home.

The ninth station brings the pilgrims over the now familiar path of prayers and ritual. Each step of bare feet on the still unfriendly stones is a reminder that it is nearly over. Each prayer and plea for all the special intentions is renewed with persistent fervour. A last opportunity to reflect on days just gone. Why did I come? Will I come again? There is a lot to reflect upon – three days apart, three extraordinary days – the island, the people, the prayers, the rituals, fasting, forgiveness, reconciliation and celebration.

Already there is a feeling of preparation for departure – some hurry, others delay leaving, slow to return to a faster pace where time does not allow for lingering, but instead has to be constantly filled with the bustle of daily living. The third day remains with the pilgrim until midnight of that third day when fasting is completed.

Shoes back on, the final gesture – on to the boat and the return journey has begun. Look again at Lough Derg. Note the changing colours, hear the lake water lapping and listen to the sounds that blend in this sacred, ancient place. The images and sounds of centuries, familiar to monastic inhabitants promise us eternal recovery from our daily stresses.

Pilgrimage over, going home – another journey – an opportunity for new beginnings. That deep need in all of us to go apart for a while, to take time out to reflect, repent and restore has been addressed on Lough Derg.

Lough Derg is a mystery – why does it continue to exist, to attract pilgrims and give hope? It is bleak, harsh and challenging. It is also timeless, sacred and imbued with the prayers of our ancestors to heal and restore us. In a world of instant solutions it forces the mind and spirit to slow down, contemplate, and experience calm and tranquillity provided by nothing more than being in a remote, enduring place.

On the boat there is a tangible feeling of satisfaction – for some the pilgrimage is done for another year, for others for the first time. Chat abounds, smiles, happy to know that it is completed.

Each year brings new pilgrims to Lough Derg, but on 27 June 2001 a new visitor, with roots long established on the island, came for the first time.

That day, the stillness so associated with Lough Derg was shattered by the noisy arrival of a helicopter in front of St Patrick's Basilica with a very special passenger – the Relics of St Thérèse of Lisieux. Over a thousand barefoot pilgrims witnessed this historic occasion. They had travelled from all parts of Ireland as well as from France, Sweden and Australia for this special event. Six of them shouldered the Reliquary to its place of veneration in the Basilica for the special welcome liturgy led by the Prior, Monsignor Richard Mohan.

The Relics were venerated in front of the statue of St Thérèse in St Patrick's Basilica. On the island, associated with simplicity of form and decoration, St Thérèse is one of only two statues in the Basilica. The other is St Davog, the abbot who founded the monastery at Saints' Island on Lough Derg in the fifth century. Construction work on St Patrick's Basilica began in 1925, the year of Canonisation of St Thérèse.

Every pilgrim to Lough Derg is special. From the fifth century into the third millennium they have come to pray for the healing grace to return to daily life with new awareness, new hope, reconciled with themselves, their community and God.

> What would I do
> Without prayer and sacrifice?
> They are all the strength I've got,
> The irresistible weapons
> Our Lord has granted me.
> I've proved it again and again
> they touch souls much more surely
> than any words can.
>
>   St Thérèse of Lisieux.

Our deepest fear is not that we are inadequate
Our deepest fear
Is that we are powerful beyond measure.
It is our light, not our darkness,
That most frightens us.
We ask ourselves, who am I
To be brilliant, gorgeous,
Talented and fabulous?
Actually, who are you not to be?
You are a child of God.
Your playing small doesn't serve the world,
There is nothing enlightened about shrinking
So that other people
Won't feel insecure around you.
We were born to make manifest
The glory of God that is within us.
It's not just in some of us; it's in everyone.
And as we let our own light shine,
We unconsciously give other people
Permission to do the same.
As we are liberated from our own fear,
Our presence automatically liberates others.

Marianne Williamson – 'A Return to Love'

## THE LOUGH DERG PILGRIMAGE

### ADMISSION

Pilgrims agree to undertake the Pilgrimage Exercises in bare feet and to abide by the Rules of the Pilgrimage Fast. Pilgrims must be at least 15 years of age, able to walk and kneel unaided and free from any illness aggravated by fasting. Warm and waterproof clothing is recommended.

### NOT PERMITTED AT LOUGH DERG

Food, sweets and chewing gum
Alcoholic and non-alcoholic drinks
Cameras, mobile phones, radios and personal stereos
Musical instruments and games
Articles and literature to sell or distribute.

### CHECK IN AT RECEPTION

Proceed to the dormitory
Remove all footwear
Collect outdoor clothing, valuables, spectacles, beads, medication, waterproofs
Proceed to St Patrick's Basilica; use cloakroom nearby for all items except valuables.

First Visit? Ask for directions/assistance at any time.

## PILGRIMAGE FAST

The fast begins at 12 midnight on the first day and ends at 12 midnight on the third day.

One Lough Derg meal is allowed each day

Otherwise, a complete fast is observed from all food and drink for three days.

**LOUGH DERG MEAL:** Available from 1.15pm to 8.15pm

Day One:     Complete First Station before meal

Day Two:     Meal at any time from 1.15pm to 6.15pm
             – Black Tea/Coffee; Dry Bread/Toast/Oatcake

Day Three:   One Lough Derg Meal and mineral waters of any kind throughout the day
             – Meal (as above) and minerals to drink.

Water and Prescribed Medication allowed at all times.

Coeliacs: contact Reception re meals and receive Communion from the Chalice.

## PILGRIMAGE EXERCISES

Nine Stations are completed over three days.

Pilgrims make the Fourth to Seventh Station together in the Basilica.

Details in Order of Exercise and Order of Station (next page)

Pilgrims gather in the Basilica for Liturgy/Prayer when the bell is rung

## THE VIGIL (10.00 pm day 1 to 10.00pm day 2)

This central penitential exercise of the Pilgrimage involves staying completely and continuously awake for 24 hours.

## LOUGH DERG – PLACE OF PRAYER

The atmosphere of peace and quiet, particularly near the Basilica and Penitential Beds, is a precious part of the pilgrimage experience.

## STAFF AND COUNSELLING

Staff at Lough Derg are always available to help during the pilgrimage. Counselling is provided by a team of trained counsellors; times displayed at Reception.

## DORMITORIES

Day 1:     Locked 4.00pm – 7.30pm

Open (for pre-vigil rest and extra clothing) 7.30pm – 9.20pm

Day 2:     Open (for wash and change) 7.30am – 11.00am

Locked 11.00pm – 7.30pm

## FACILITIES

Blessed Sacrament Chapel – a place for quiet prayer.

Shop – for books, religious objects, postcards and information on Friends of Lough Derg.

There is a blessing twice daily.

First Aid Station – for medical assistance.


## HEALTH AND SAFETY

Note position of fire alarms and observe fire drill regulations in the event of emergency.

Smoking is restricted to certain areas in the interests of public safety and as a courtesy to other pilgrims.

Use litter bins provided.


## ORDER OF EXERCISES

First Day

| | |
|---|---|
| 12.00 midnight | Begin Fast |
| | Pilgrims arrive as early as possible |
| | (any day from 1 June to 13 August), register and await boat. |
| | Boats: 10.30am until 3.00pm |
| | |
| 11.00 am | Begin Station. Complete Three Stations before 9.15pm |
| 6.30pm | Opening Mass |
| 9.20pm | Night Prayer and Benediction |

The Vigil

| | |
|---|---|
| 10.15pm | Introduction to Vigil |
| 11.45pm | Rosary |
| 12.30am | Fourth Station |
| 2.00am | Fifth Station |
| 3.30am | Sixth Station |
| 5.00am | Seventh Station |
| 6.30am | Morning Mass |
| 8.30am | Sacrament of Reconciliation followed by Eighth Station |
| 12.00 noon | Renewal of Baptismal Promises |
| 3.00pm | Way of the Cross |
| 6.30pm | Evening Mass |
| 9.20pm | Night Prayer and Benediction |
| 10.00pm | Conclusion of Vigil |

Third Day

| | |
|---|---|
| 6.00am | Bell for rising |
| 6.30am | Closing Mass |
| 7.30am | Ninth Station |
| 9.45am | Departure of boats |

## ORDER OF STATIONS

Begin the Station with a visit to the Blessed Sacrament in St Patrick's Basilica.

Go to St Patrick's Cross near the Basilica; kneel, and say one Our Father, one Hail Mary and one Creed. Kiss the Cross

Go to St Brigid's Cross on the outside wall of the Basilica; kneel and say three Our Fathers, three Hail Marys and one Creed. With your back to the Cross, stand with arms fully outstretched, and say three times, 'I renounce the World, the Flesh, and the Devil'.

Walk slowly, by your right hand, four times around the Basilica, while praying silently seven decades of the Rosary and one Creed at the end.

Go to St Brigid's Bed. (If there is a queue, please join it before going to the Bed.)
At the bed:
  (a)  walk three times around the outside, by your right hand, while saying three Our Fathers, three Hail Marys and one Creed;
  (b)  kneel at the entrance to the Bed and repeat these prayers;
  (c)  walk three times around the inside and say these prayers again;
  (d)  kneel at the Cross in the centre and say these prayers for the fourth time.
Repeat these exercises at:
  St Brendan's Bed
  St Catherine's Bed
  St Columba's Bed

Walk six times around the outside of the large Penitential Bed, which comprises St Patrick's Bed and that of Sts Davog and Molaise, while saying six Our Fathers, six Hail Marys and One Creed.

Kneel at the entrance to St Patrick's Bed and say three Our Fathers, three Hail Marys and one Creed. Walk three times around the inside while repeating these prayers. Kneel at the Cross in the centre and say them again.

Kneel at the entrance to the Bed of Sts Davog and Molaise and say three Our Fathers, three Hail Marys and one Creed. Walk three times around the inside while repeating these prayers. Kneel at the Cross in the centre and say them again.

Go to the water's edge; stand and say five Our Fathers, five Hail Marys and one Creed. Kneel and repeat these prayers. Make the Sign of the Cross with lake water as a reminder of your Baptism.

Return to St Patrick's Cross; kneel and say one Our Father, one Hail Mary and one Creed.

Go to the Basilica and conclude the Station by reciting Psalm 15 or by saying five Our Fathers, five Hail Marys and one Creed, for the Pope's intentions.

THE APOSTLES' CREED
    I believe in God, the Father almighty,
    creator of heaven and earth.
    I believe in Jesus Christ, his only Son, our Lord.
    He was conceived by the power of the Holy Spirit,
    and born of the Virgin Mary.
    He suffered under Pontius Pilate,
    was crucified, died and was buried.
    He descended to the dead.
    On the third day he rose again.
    He ascended into heaven,
    and is seated at the right hand of the Father.
    He will come again to judge the living and the dead.
    I believe in the Holy Spirit,
    the holy Catholic Church, the communion of saints,
    the forgiveness of sins,
    the resurrection of the body,
    and life everlasting. Amen.

PSALM 15
    Preserve me, God, I take refuge in you.
    I say to the Lord: You are my God.
    My happiness lies in you alone.

    He has put into my heart a marvellous love
    for the faithful ones who dwell on his land.
    Those who choose other gods increase their sorrows.

Never will I offer their offerings of blood.
Never will I take their name upon my lips.

O Lord, it is you who are my portion and cup;
it is you yourself who are my prize.
The lot marked out for me is my delight:
welcome indeed the heritage that falls to me!

I will bless the Lord who gives me counsel,
who even at night directs my heart.
I keep the Lord ever in my sight:
since he is at my right hand, I shall stand firm.

And so my heart rejoices, my soul is glad;
even my body shall rest in safety.
For you will not leave my soul among the dead,
nor let your beloved know decay.

You will show me the path of life,
the fullness of joy in your presence,
at your right hand happiness for ever.